Rest & Resilience

Following the Way of Jesus through Lent

THE BETHANY FELLOWS

Edited by MELANIE HARRELL DELANEY, LAUREN BENNETT & DARREN W. PHELPS

chalice
PRESS

Print: 9780827233201   EPUB: 9780827233218

EPDF: 9780827233225

ChalicePress.com

Printed in the United States of America

Table of Contents

Rest and Resilience: The Bethany Way

How do you know spring is coming in your little corner of the world?

Here in my hometown, most of the natural world loses its color for the winter season. Branches are bare, the sky is gray, and the ground is brown or white (or even worse, brownish-white as the snow and mud mix together). While Christmas lights add a delightful pop of color for a time, even the most persistent among us have typically turned off these little strings of joy by the beginning of February, their light packed away even while the nights are still long. I spend much of these in-between months yearning for the bright delight of summer, the colorful displays of health and life. I can remember how the sun feels in the vibrant times, the richness of spring blooms, and I watch for "the first green of spring" with vigilance.

Two years ago in the fall, my father, children, and I planted a tree in our backyard. It will someday be a beautiful magnolia, with star-like blossoms. I imagine watching the tree grow taller alongside my kids, the memory of planting the tree with my father a sacred one. Last spring, my daughter and I watched the bare branches with anticipation. Had the little sapling survived the winter? We kept vigil for weeks, ready to celebrate the first bud or hint of spring growth, disappointed when nothing happened. "I don't think the tree made it, Dad," I said in the middle of May. "The branches look dead. There isn't even a spot of green. I don't think the tree survived." What I didn't say was, "This tree can't die, because I have *expectations!*"

But wouldn't you know, the tree wasn't dead! It was dormant and still, resting and preparing for the right season of growth. But oh, how I wanted to rush it along. We had *life* to live, after all!

The season of Lent can feel like a dormant time in the Christian rhythm. Six whole weeks of introspection, repentance, sacrifice … and do I really have to give up my love of baked goods? (No? Ok, good!) No matter the path, these weeks leading up to Easter are typically a little sparse, a little less colorful; each week can feel quite long as we eagerly anticipate the joy of Easter resurrection. Some of us wish we could skip the slower seasons of church and spiritual life altogether. We need some *resurrection* around here, you know?

Jesus knows there is holy work to be done in the world. There are relationships to mend, political divides to bridge, global wars to resolve, environmental healing to attend to, justice to bring about, and people to feed, clothe, and shelter. In scripture, Jesus says, "the poor will always be with you"

(Matthew 26:11), and although we continue to work toward wholeness for all, he is right. We are in this for the long haul, friends.

So how do we survive the long winters? How do we sustain our response, as people of faith, with so many crises in the world and so many neighbors in need?

We rest. We nap. We sing, dance, create, and breathe. We take long, meandering walks through the lonely, bare woods. Or we sit in silence, producing nothing. We pray the Psalms, listen to the breeze, watch water move, plant a seed.

Really, you ask? Do we have *time* for all of that?

And I ask, do we have time *not* to?

In scripture, Jesus does a *lot* of powerful ministry in his short embodied life. He heals the sick, feeds the hungry, transforms religious practices and people's hearts and minds. Jesus worked miracle after miracle. He changed the world. And yet, he also knew when to rest. He knew when to seek solitude and stillness as he listened for God's voice; when to be vulnerable; when to cry and when to laugh; when to return to his sacred community; how to see the world with creative vision and new hope; and how to bring all of us along with him in resilient faith. Many times in scripture, Jesus' moments of renewal and resilience are rooted in a small town built on a hillside—the town of Bethany.

This book of devotions follows Jesus' journey as it weaves in and out of Bethany, just two miles outside of Jerusalem. Bethany is where a few of Jesus' good friends lived, where he was able to rest and be vulnerable, to be anointed and healed himself, and to pray and prepare for difficult ministry ahead (including the journey toward Jerusalem on Palm Sunday). Each week of this Lenten series begins with an experience Jesus had in Bethany and offers a practice of rest and renewal modeled after Jesus' own way.

The authors of these devotions are all current Bethany Fellows or alumni. Bethany Fellows is an ecumenical ministry rooted in the Christian Church (Disciples of Christ), serving congregations by helping young pastors transition from seminary to sustained ministry with wellbeing and strength of spirit. Bethany Fellows is a community of prayer, supportive colleagues, wise mentors, and contemplative spiritual practices. We offer small-group support and joyful retreats that include worship, wise practice, prayer, play, creativity, and renewal for pastors so they can lead with wisdom, courage, and resilience.

Each weekly theme in this devotion journey is a core practice of what we call, "The Bethany Way," a rhythm of life and leadership modeled after

Jesus' pattern of returning to Bethany for rest, prayer, connection, healing, and preparation for the next phase of ministry. As pastors, we have found this rhythm to be deeply life-giving, and we trust it will be so for you as well, as you navigate seasons of your own faith journey.

Two years after planting the young tree with my dad, I knew to wait patiently. I didn't even check for new growth until March! Again, I was devastated. A neighboring deer had chomped the dormant branches as an early-spring snack. The little branches were broken off near the ground and stripped bare of their protective bark. This, certainly, would mean the end of our beloved tree. I wept. And still, months later than I expected in the spring, small green leaves appeared. Our little magnolia is resilient! She wasn't dead, just preparing. She will surely bloom someday—she just knows to take a good, long, rest first.

—Rev. Melanie Harrell Delaney
co-director/pastor, Bethany Fellows

Prepare

Spiritual Practice Invitation

Create a sacred space for your Lenten journey.
Will your space include a candle, journal, or other sacred objects?

At the beginning of each week, you will be invited to explore a spiritual practice in rhythm with the theme of the week. Consider adopting this practice for the week or the entire season.

Prepare

When he had come near Bethphage and Bethany, at the place called the Mount of Olives, he sent two of the disciples, saying, "Go into the village ahead of you..." (Luke 19:29–30a, NRSV)

I imagine Jesus standing on the quiet hillside of the Mount of Olives, on the edge of Bethany and Bethphage, looking out toward the horizon where the bustling city of Jerusalem lay sprawling. What was he feeling? Jesus was preparing to enter the city the next day (the day we know as Palm Sunday). We know how the story goes: Crowds cheering and waving palm branches at the start of a parade that eventually leads Jesus to the cross. I wonder if Jesus took a slow, deep breath just then, beginning a series of preparations for what lay ahead. Two of his disciples went off to the city to look for a colt for Jesus to ride. But Jesus stayed back. What did he do then? Did he find a shady spot to sit and pray with the remaining disciples? Did he go back and nap at the home of Mary and Martha, waiting for word that the disciples had returned with the colt? Did he go for a walk, the rhythm of his footsteps a moving meditation?

Today marks the first day of the season of Lent, a time of spiritual preparation, reflection, and repentance leading up to Easter. These forty days are an invitation to a slower pace. These days are a gift, in which blessings await through intentional time with God, your spiritual community, and your own heart.

How will you prepare for this time? How will you mark the beginning of your journey of intention? With worship? With prayer and repentance? By setting an intention to rest?

Prayer: Create in me a clean heart, O God, and renew a right spirit within me. Do not cast me away from your presence, and do not take your holy spirit from me. Restore to me the joy of your salvation, and sustain in me a willing spirit (Psalm 51:10–12).

—Rev. Melanie Harrell Delaney

Asleep In My Ashes

Restore to me the joy of your salvation and sustain in me a willing spirit. (Psalm 51:12, NRSV)

I attended a retreat in a remote, forested stretch of Michigan's Upper Peninsula on Lake Superior. We were welcomed with the story of native guides leading explorers. After days of rigorous travel, the explorers were up at dawn, ready to press on, but the guides demurred, saying, "We will go no further today. We're waiting for our souls to catch up to us."

The Lenten journey has begun, but we will go no further today. Lest we plunge headlong into a checklist of Lenten to-dos, we do well to pause first. Give yourself permission to rest. Rest and pray. Pray with the psalmist for your spirit to be sustained throughout these forty days and joyfully restored at season's end.

Running late for the 6 p.m. Ash Wednesday service last year, my wife and I slid into our seats just in time for the call to worship. Over the next hour, thanks to the tranquil, slow-moving liturgy of scripture, music, and prayer, I felt myself slowing down, settling in. We walked forward, received the ashes on our foreheads, and left in soothing silence. We drove home for dinner and, after a quiet evening, went to bed.

In the morning, I looked in the mirror and, smiling, saw the ashes were still on my forehead. I had slept in my ashes and awoke rested and restored. Joy! I had done nothing but slow down and rest … and that was a gracious plenty.

Prayer: Lord God, give us willing spirits for this Lenten journey, holy rest along the way, and a joyous restoration at journey's end.

—Rev. David A. Shirey

Don't Rush

Be still, and know that I am God! (Psalm 46:10, NRSV)

In the Children Worship & Wonder program developed by Sonja Stewart and Jerome Berryman, children are taught how to prepare for worship. The storyteller begins by saying, "In this place we have all the time we need. So, we don't need to hurry." We teach children these things, but by the time we reach adulthood, we have forgotten them ourselves. We forget to take our time; we forget to put aside the rush of the world around us and to let the stories of Jesus fill us, to feel the nearness of God.

We have entered the Lenten season. A season marked by ash on our forehead, a physical reminder of our frailty, a reminder to be gentle with ourselves, a reminder that we cannot rush, a reminder to embrace the stillness.

As we prepare ourselves for this sacred season that is marked by deep listening, vulnerability, and connection, may we also remember that it is a season to be still, to know that God is among us, to quiet our bodies and our minds. May we know that here in this season, we have time to still our bodies, to breathe slowly and abide intentionally. We can be gentle with ourselves as we attend to the divine presence among us.

Prayer: Holy One, as we follow Jesus on this journey, may we know the beauty of slowing down. May we find you in the stillness. Amen.

—Rev. Cheryl Russell Kunkel

Toddler Consciousness

I am about to do a new thing; now it springs forth; do you not perceive it? I will make a way in the wilderness and rivers in the desert. (Isaiah 43:19, NRSV)

As we prepare ourselves for this season of reflection and rest, we are invited to remember our habitual tendency to perceive the world around us in ways that are limiting and limited.

Psychologist Alison Gopnick reflected on an adult walking to the corner to pick up some milk, and considered how adults might learn from children. She wrote, "going for a walk with a 2-year-old is like going for a walk with William Blake," because as an adult if you go to the corner store to get milk, and you have been on this block many times, and you have become habituated, "it kind of disappears from your consciousness."[1]

> But if you do the same walk with a two-year-old, you realize, wait a minute. This, three blocks, it's just amazing. It's so rich. There's dogs and there's gates and there's pizza fliers and there's plants and trees and there's airplanes.[2]

What might we need in this season to be more open to awe, to see the world around us anew, with an open awareness to all the dogs and plants and people and clouds and rivers in the desert?

God is ready to do a new thing within and among us. Are we ready to perceive it?

Prayer: Holy One, open our eyes to perceive your presence. Help us to slow down enough to notice. Kindle delight in our hearts when we realize that even a tiny corner of your creation is full of new things to see. Help us experience awe in the everyday. Prepare our hearts, minds, bodies, and spirits to be open to you in this sacred season of rest. Amen.

—Rev. Tiffany Curtis

---

[1] Klein, Ezra, narrator. "Why Adults Lose the 'Beginner's Mind.'" *The Ezra Klein Show, The New York Times* (April 16 2021). https://www.nytimes.com/2021/04/16/opinion/ezra-klein-podcast-alison-gopnik.html?

[2] Ibid.

WEEK 1

Rest

Spiritual Practice Invitation:

Take a nap.

Don't feel guilty about it. It's your spiritual practice!

At the beginning of each week, you will be invited to explore a spiritual practice in rhythm with the theme of the week. Consider adopting this practice for the week or the entire season.

The Call to Rest

When the religious leaders saw the outrageous things Jesus was doing, and heard all the children running and shouting through the Temple, "Hosanna to David's Son!" they were up in arms and took Jesus to task. "Do you hear what these children are saying? Jesus said, "Yes, I hear them. And haven't you read in God's Word, 'From the mouths of children and babies I'll furnish a place of praise'?" Fed up, Jesus spun around and left the city for Bethany, where he spent the night. (Matthew 21:15–17, The Message)

In Matthew 21 we see Jesus expressing holy outrage. After his prophetic ministry, while attempting to retreat, Jesus experienced, in the temple, what had become a place of thieves. This is the last place one would expect to witness any mistreatment to God's people ... in the temple.

Have you experienced a season of deep exhaustion? Daily, our lives are compacted and complicated with rules, goals, difficult decisions, and balancing self-care. We are challenged with loving people who are not kind or who view the world quite differently. In today's scripture passage, the religious leaders wanted Jesus to "do something" about the children running about the temple. Jesus may have been tempted to engage in a long debate. Instead, he chose his actions with intention. Expressing his holy outrage, he "spun around" from the argument, returning to Bethany, a place of rest and renewal.

Rest is holy! The simplicity of the practice is nourishing to our souls and to our bodies. It is not surprising that we witness Jesus' desire to retreat. Rest was a priority. During the Lenten season, we are invited to seek sacred spaces to rest. Places of oneness and silence with God. Places where we can breathe and welcome the Holy Spirit to refresh our souls.

Prayer: Dear God, when my schedule becomes hectic or when I'm feeling overwhelmed, lead me to the sacred place to be one with you. Show me the power of rest. May it give life to my daily journey.

—Rev. Dr. Darren Phelps

Rest in the Storm

A great windstorm arose, and the waves beat into the boat, so that the boat was already being swamped. But [Jesus] was in the stern, asleep on the cushion. (Mark 4:38, NRSV)

Jesus took naps. This is information about Jesus that I have always loved, and not only because I am an adoring fan of the napping pastime. The incarnate, fully human, God-with-us Jesus experienced fatigue, exhaustion, and the physical necessity of sleep just as we do. Yet, it seems that Jesus did not limit his snoozing to lazy Sabbath afternoons and retreats to the city of Bethany. He managed to sleep soundly on a boat amid a seemingly life-threatening storm!

It is ideal and beneficial to get away on occasion for extended Sabbath rest and renewal, particularly after demanding, busy, or difficult seasons. However, life does not always allow for such spaciousness; nor does a yearly retreat or vacation provide the revitalization necessary for sustenance and wellbeing the remainder of the year. So, how can you press reset when you find yourself stuck in the middle of life's storms? What Sabbath practices and rhythms keep you anchored to the peace of Christ when the world around you is anything but peaceful?

Your Sabbath anchors may be as unique as you are. Here are mine:

- breathing deeply;
- remaining attentive to God's always-abiding presence and activity;
- expressing gratitude;
- meditating on God's Word;
- playing and delighting in the gifts of God;
- and never underestimating the power of a good nap!

Prayer: Creator God, still the troubled waters of our souls. Come to our aid when we cry out in fear. May we experience your presence and power in stillness and silence, as well as in the fury of life's storms. Anchor us to the peace of Christ and renew within us a faithful, steadfast spirit. Amen.

—Rev. Casey Tanguay

Rest

Jesus said to them, "Come away to a deserted place all by yourselves and rest a while." For many were coming and going, and they had no leisure even to eat. (Mark 6:31, NRSV)

The disciples came to tell Jesus about all of the work they had been doing. Jesus invited them to take some time off together, to find a deserted, solitary space, and to rest a while. On their way to a solitary space, crowds of people followed them and were in need of help. Jesus, having compassion on the crowd, then put the disciples to work.

The disciples tried to remind Jesus that he had told them to rest. Again, Jesus put the disciples to work. "Go, feed the crowd." The disciples did as Jesus asked, and the crowd was fed with plenty of leftovers. But what about Jesus' invitation for the disciples to rest? Maybe the disciples' rest occurred on the boat ride to the solitary place. Maybe they enjoyed the communal silence and beauty of creation as they traveled. Maybe their rest occurred while sitting down and eating with the crowd.

The idea of rest in this text is a brief break from labor or a moment of refreshing. Like the disciples, there are times in our lives when we cannot get away for a week or a weekend, but we can take moments of intentional rest throughout the day or week. Rest can be simple.

We can practice mindfulness in our work, which will allow us to really see those we are serving. We can be intentional about enjoying the time between the events of the day; driving in silence between events or sitting in silence between zoom calls.

Prayer: God, show me the daily moments when I can enter into your rest.

—Rev. Larry J. Morris III

The Rest of Your Life

But those who wait for the Lord shall renew their strength, they shall mount up with wings like eagles, they shall run and not be weary, they shall walk and not faint. (Isaiah 40:31, NRSV)

Sometimes we don't choose rest, it chooses us. I will never forget the summer when a health emergency led to a six-week medical leave from pastoring my church. Resting meant canceling "all the things" to allow time for the deep rest my mind/body/spirit needed.

I remember the first time I went for a walk on a sunny afternoon following surgery. I started by walking barefoot outside on the soft green grass in the yard. The second day I walked down the driveway. The third day I walked halfway down the block.

Each day I grew a little bit stronger. I rested better after the walks. The resting became a time of waiting for my strength to return.

I discovered my life's wellbeing depended on the quality of my rest. The medical leave turned out to be a surprising gift. My job was simply to be and to rest.

But don't wait to have a medical emergency to get the restorative rest your mind/body/spirit crave. What would it look like to take time for rest before we are pushed to the point of illness? What would it look like to create rhythms of deep rest for our weary bones?

As a recovering workaholic who regularly made myself sick with migraines, I am now learning to patiently wait for the Lord. I have no more migraines. I am learning to put my rest in God.

Prayer: God, help us to wait for you. God, help us to rest in you. God, help us make time for the rest of our lives. Amen.

—Rev. Dr. Sarah Griffith Lund

Wide Open Spaces

He brought me out into a spacious place; he rescued me because he delighted in me. (Psalm 18:19, NIV)

I stay too busy. My Google Calendar looks like a game of Tetris gone wrong, blocks of time stacked on each other, too many appointments crammed next to each other.

I'm working on it. I swear. But sometimes my to-do list seems fuller at the end of the week than it did at the beginning.

When this happens, the simple practice of spending time in an open space slows my mind and mends my soul. It helps me breathe deeper, focus my vision on things farther away than the nearest screen, and reminds me that my anxious deadlines are often self-imposed expectations.

That's why I love these words from Psalm 18. The Psalmist covers many of the usual themes—trusting, waiting, and calling on God—but the deliverance of being brought "into a spacious place" is biblically one of a kind. How many of us just need some room to breathe?

I live next to a cornfield. Sometimes I stand at the edge and stare at the expanse, gazing at the cloud formations until I feel holy peace rescue and reorient me.

So, where are your spacious places? God delights in you and will rescue you with rest.

Prayer: Holy one, rescue us—usually from our own anxieties and expectations. Let our hearts open to your expansive grace and remember the shared delight that it is to be your beloved child. Amen.

—Rev. Steve Mason

The Littlest Commandment

That is why the Lord blessed the Sabbath day and made it holy. (Exodus 20:11b, CEB)

When considering the "big ten" handed down to Moses, I often refer to keeping Sabbath as the littlest commandment, the one so many of us ignore. Notice: The good work of creation was only complete when God rested. God loves us so much God models rest taking for us. Jesus rested and used the Sabbath to bring love and life into the world, even when others threatened him for those efforts.

One powerful way to reject the sin of the world is by insisting on rest. Prioritize rest in your life. Don't leave it to spare moments that vanish away. Claim them as essential to your health and your community's health. Fight for the right of others to rest, to bring life to your family, any employees, refugees, even animals. Respect our Maker, who didn't need to rest but chose to. Like our Creator, we complete our work of love when we rest.

Prayer: Gracious Creator, help us to cherish the blessing of rest in our lives and in the lives of all our neighbors. Amen.

—Rev. Isaac Varner

Sabbath Moments

Come to me, all you who are weary and burdened, and I will give you rest. (Matthew 11:28, NRSV)

I have often said, "Sabbath is not a suggestion. It is a commandment." But what happens when you can't rest the way God intended? What happens when you want to keep the Sabbath but your livelihood doesn't allow for it?

Until recently, I spent almost ten years in seasonal work at Christian summer camps. From Memorial Day to mid-August, I rarely got a day off. I definitely didn't get a Sabbath every seventh day and I didn't make it to church. I'm not the only one.

There are loads of people in this world who can't keep the sabbath every seven days—the single mom who works three jobs, the caretaker of a cancer patient, the bi-vocational pastor who preaches on his or her day off. Oil rigs don't stop for the Sabbath; neither does the harvest ... or pandemics.

How do you keep the Sabbath when your work doesn't allow you to rest for an entire day? I look to scripture as a guide. I remember that Jesus snuck away for Sabbath moments in the bottom of boats, on the top of mountains, and by himself in prayer. He can be the source of my spiritual rest, even when physical rest may not be possible. I find quiet Sabbath moments to pause, breathe, sing, pray, and start again. I remember that Jesus grabbed moments of rest when he could. I grab a Sabbath moment and thank God for a breath, and I look forward to when a time of real rest will come.

If you are weary, you are not alone.

Prayer: Dear God, thank you for Sabbath moments. Help us to notice them, and help them sustain us for now. Amen.

—Rev. Tiff Williams

WEEK 2

Listen

Spiritual Practice Invitation:

Find a comfortable place to sit without distraction.
Set a timer for two minutes (or five or twenty).
Close your eyes. Pay attention to your breath. Listen to your heart.

At the beginning of each week, you will be invited to explore a spiritual practice in rhythm with the theme of the week. Consider adopting this practice for the week or the entire season.

Listen Deeper

She had a sister named Mary, who sat at the Lord's feet and listened to what he was saying. (Luke 10:39, NRSV)

"What do you hear?" the naturalist asked our group as we stood on a well-worn path in the middle of the woods. I took a deep breath and closed my eyes, focusing on the sounds around me: first, the loud crunch of gravel as my neighbor fidgeted in place, and a quieter sniffle further down. I could hear the energy of our efforts to be still. Then, birdsong ... a frog and a cicada adding a steady thrum. I was surprised by how much I could hear (and the volume of it all!) in what moments ago had seemed like quiet, empty woods.

"Now try it again," the naturalist urged. "This time, go deeper. Listen for what is beyond the sound."

We couldn't imagine what else we would hear, but we did it anyway. Gravel. Sniffle. Birdsong. Frog. Cicada. All still there in rhythm as before. "Listen deeper..." What else was there? I took another breath, and as I got to the base of the exhale, I held it there. The stillness of my chest took my attention to a stillness underneath the sounds. The subtle breeze, a feather-whisper. The pulse of tree roots interconnected under my feet, inaudible to my ear, yet audible to my heart. Indeed, a silent and holy chorus could be heard with time, stillness, and a second listen.

Today, take a moment to stop and listen. What do you hear? Listen for the first sounds that your ears pick up, and then listen for what is beneath, beyond. Hold silence for two to three minutes. What does your heart hear in the silence?

Prayer: Holy One, as I settle my body and my breath, whisper your wisdom to me. Remind me to hold this sacred space, to pay attention to your presence, and to rest in your love. Amen.

—Rev. Melanie Harrell Delaney

Ears to Hear

Let anyone with ears to hear listen! (Luke 8:8b, NRSV)

What is the difference between hearing and listening? The words may seem to mean the same thing, but there is an intentionality to listening that is not present in hearing. In our loud, chaotic world there are a multitude of noises around us all the time. We hear them, but we don't necessarily listen to them.

Jesus uses the phrase, "Let anyone with ears to hear listen" at least seven times in the gospels. It's a call to pay attention to what he is saying, and not just with our ears. We cannot physically hear his voice, but we can still listen to his words. It takes intentionality on our part to filter out the background and focus on what matters. It takes time and energy to truly listen to what Jesus is telling us. That is how we become the good soil, ready to listen to that word and bear fruit.

Prayer: Lord of cacophony and of silence, help us to discern your word in the noisiness of this world so that we may grow in you, and you in us. Amen.

—Rev. Jack Knox

Hear and Follow

My sheep hear my voice. I know them, and they follow me. (John 10:27, NRSV)

"What is yours to do?"

The question, asked by a trusted confidant, cut through the mental chaos in a way nothing else had. Expectations, fears, anger, and hope had been swirling around and tumbling out of my mouth for who knows how long. As I tried to make sense of a difficult situation, the wisdom of that one question slowed the swirling thoughts and stopped my verbal processing.

In that moment, I heard the voice of God in the words of a friend. I was invited to respond to God's voice and follow a healthier and more sustainable path—a redirection requiring thoughtfulness and difficult decisions, but a path that was holy and faithful.

The voices of this world—voices of fear and hate, of temptation and greed—join the cacophony of our own pain and desires. They can make it difficult to hear the voice of God, to attend to the holy wisdom of others. But it is there, calling us by name, redirecting us, and leading us as the Good Shepherd.

Prayer: Guiding Love, may we attend to the wisdom of the Good Shepherd, recognize God's voice, and follow faithfully. Amen.

—Rev. Sarah Kingsbery

Flock

They will listen to my voice and there will be one flock, with one shepherd. (John 10:16, NIV)

Sermons about this text often focus on the relationship between Christians and Christ. The movement goes like this: The sheep learn the tone and tenor of the shepherd's voice through the shepherd's leading, prodding, and care. It's the same for Christians. We learn the voice of our Lord through proximity and time as we respond to God's leading, prodding, and care.

But other sheep in another fold know the voice of the same shepherd. Jesus says there will be one flock with one shepherd. In speaking about himself as the good shepherd, Jesus provides a vision for the unity of the church—unity but not uniformity. When we grow accustomed to the voice of Jesus, we will also become accustomed to the presence of people unlike us. As we walk with and grow in our relationship with Jesus, we realize that we do not walk alone but with all who hear and follow his voice.

The one flock is a beautiful image—the one body united in the beautiful rainbow that is God's church. We know the lived reality of the church isn't there yet, and we realize how far we have to go. Yet, we who follow the voice of our shepherd are on a journey toward resurrection. This is the season to listen to and follow our shepherd's voice. In the listening and the following, may we become more open to the voice and presence of our neighbors in the flock.

Prayer: Shepherding God, you call and we listen, you lead and we follow. We do not do this alone. As we journey toward a world made new, may we continue to be surprised at the wide circles of your welcome. Amen.

—Rev. Nathan Kibler

Undivided Attention

As Jesus and his disciples were on their way, he came to a village where a woman named Martha opened her home to him. She had a sister called Mary, who sat at the Lord's feet listening to what he said. But Martha was distracted by all the preparations that had to be made. (Luke 10: 38–40a, AMP)

Our two-year-old was nowhere to be found. We had been calling for him and looking for him both inside and outside of our house. At the point of terror and desperation, I heard a tiny voice from behind some curtains.

"I'm here."

After what felt like an eternity, but in reality was probably fifteen minutes, our quiet little boy made his presence known and was found. Sometimes to hear something holy—a poetic sermon, advice from a colleague, words of worry or sadness from a friend, or a still, small voice reminding us of God's presence—we need to slow down long enough to listen.

We have so many reasons to be distracted or not pay attention to the obvious messages, let alone a divine presence. Some listen like Mary, with our full and undivided attention, sitting at Jesus' feet, hanging on every word. Some of us are keeping busy with the many preparations, and cleaning, like Martha. Listening allows us to see deeper into another's heart. Only then can we offer the help and hope they need. Each time we pray, we are gifted with God's undivided attention.

Prayer: Dear God, thank you for listening. Thank you for listening, even when we might be overwhelmed with our busyness or worried about what comes next. Thank you for being this gift of the perfect listener. Amen

—Rev. Sara Wilcox Patty

Tune Out to Tune In

But Martha was distracted with much serving ...
(Luke 10:40 NKJV)

Distractions—small, large, unexpected. They are all around us.

They show up at what seems like the wrong time. Yet, at other times, we welcome them.

Some distractions are apparent. Others are not as easily recognizable, but that doesn't negate their existence.

Martha was distracted in a dual kind of way. The text speaks of her initial distraction as much as her serving. I can't say I blame her. After all, it was Jesus who'd come to visit. We'd all want Jesus to come to a clean home and do our best to serve Him well.

The second distraction is not as noticeable, but it exists. Martha was distracted by Mary's *in*action. She was distracted by the fact that Mary was listening to Jesus. Mary was so in tune to what Jesus was saying, she was unbothered by Martha.

Distractions—they are all around us. Yet we have options on how to deal with distractions. We can tune in to them and see where they lead, or we can tune them out and listen.

What do you want to *tune-in* to?

What distractions do you need to *tune out*, so that you can hear the heart of God?

Prayer: Lord, sometimes the noise of life and the world can be so loud. Help us to quiet our souls, so that we may hear you. Amen.

—Rev. Rae Karim

WEEK 3

Vulnerable

Spiritual Practice Invitation:

Create something—visual art, a meal, a poem, a letter—and give it away.

At the beginning of each week, you will be invited to explore a spiritual practice in rhythm with the theme of the week. Consider adopting this practice for the week or the entire season.

Bear It All

She has done a beautiful thing... (Matthew 26:10, ESV)

You've been there. The moment you say or do something courageous and another person questions you. The opposition might come from a look or—the worst—through audible verbal challenge. Suddenly, your pulse quickens, your skin flushes, and you ask yourself, "Why am I doing this? Is it right? Should I back out?"

I wonder what went through Mary's mind as she poured out the equivalent of twelve ounces of expensive perfume on the feet of Jesus. When she opened the jar and the smell of nard interrupted whatever conversation was undoubtedly happening, did she start sweating, knowing people were paying attention? Did she question her decision to pour out this perfume? Where did she even get it? Was it a gift passed down from a grandmother, was the jar purchased after a long season of saving resources or filled slowly over time, even generations? Did she wonder if she was doing right with her resources when she was challenged in front of everyone?

Later in the week, when Judas betrayed Jesus with a kiss, did they both smell that nard and think back to that moment of extravagant love? Did Judas regret what he was about to do even then? Did Jesus wonder if he could actually face murder with dignity?

Every act of courage invites internal questioning and embodied responses, revealing our vulnerability, exposing our insecurities, and demanding strength to live into the questions. Indeed, every act of courageous love that is questioned from within or from the outside draws us nearer to the proclamation with which Jesus blesses Mary, "You have done a beautiful thing."

Prayer: Courageous God, thank you for meeting us in our questions and joining us when we feel most vulnerable. Interrupt us with reminders of love so that we will be bearers of extravagant beauty, generosity, and joy, especially when we are flooded with insecurities. Open our senses as we join in your unfinished work to courageously bear it all in love. Amen.

—Rev. Lauren Bennett

Resisting Vulnerability

Nicodemus came to Jesus at night and said, "Rabbi, we know that you are a teacher who has come from God. For no one could perform the signs you are doing if God were not with him." (John 3:2, NIV)

Cost–benefit analysis is pervasive in our lives. Every purchase and decision we face is an opportunity for us to enter some level of cost–benefit analysis. Do the benefits outweigh the cost? Is it worth it?

I grew up in a rural Midwestern town and was well aware of the cost–benefit analysis of self-reflection and vulnerability. I was well aware that the cost of this self-reflection work was too high for the minimal benefit it could return. "No good can come of it," was the phrase I heard again and again as I grew up. I imagine many have similar stories about self-reflection and vulnerability. And I imagine many have resisted opportunities for vulnerability and self-reflection because of this way of thinking.

I am not sure if Nicodemus would have used the economic language of cost–benefit analysis, but I do believe he knew that he was taking a great risk in visiting Jesus under the cover of night. His reputation and status in the community were at stake. The potential cost was too high to meet with this man who had just cleansed the temple of the moneychangers. "No good can come of it."

Here's the thing about cost–benefit analysis. If you're relying on incomplete or inaccurate data, the results of the analysis will follow suit. The "no good can come of it" way of thinking focuses too much on the cost and ignores the benefits. Vulnerability and self-reflection have incredible benefits—just as Nicodemus visiting Jesus had incredible benefits. It resulted in John 3:16, that great summary of the Good News. Instead of resisting vulnerability, let us adopt Nicodemus's approach of curiosity and allow ourselves to think, "MUCH good WILL come of it."

Prayer: Beneficent God, encourage us to find opportunities for self-reflection and vulnerability. Walk with us as we go about this work so that much good will come of it. Amen.

—Rev. Seth Rash

When Weeping Isn't Enough

Jesus wept. (John 11:35, NIV)

The shortest verse in the scriptures is, "Jesus wept." I hate crying—the headache, dry eyes, snot-clogged throat. But I hate it most because it requires vulnerability. For years, I believed that vulnerability was weakness. But I was wrong and am wrong every time I forget that Jesus, too, wept.

Vulnerability doesn't come naturally to me. I've spent years learning how to make space for vulnerability, not just with God and others but with myself. Allowing the space for the power of all types of emotions is a difficult task for the church.

Congregations are places we go when we need to weep, but they need to be safe for all kinds of moments of vulnerability. For moments of fear, doubt, learning, transition, wrong-doing, embarrassment, innovation, joy, and hope. *Jesus wept.* But Mary put all her hope in the Lord, in a grand gesture of faith in a room of Jesus' closest followers. Mary, an outsider. She became vulnerable to share her faith with the world. To stand up and say, "For you Christ, I surrender."

Prayer: God of safety, help me to render myself to you, to surrender to you, to be vulnerable going forward. Amen.

—Rev. Aerii Smith

Give Us Today, Our Daily Bread

If you love me, you will keep my commandments. And I will ask [God] to send you another Advocate and to be with you forever—the Spirit of [T]ruth ... you know [God] because [God] abides with you. (John 14:15–17, NIV)

"I cannot ask for your forgiveness, for what has happened cannot be forgiven. But know that I am truly sorry." My newborn daughter's surgeon uttered these words before painstakingly walking us step-by-step through the surgery that left our child recovering from a heart attack and stroke.

Raw, gut wrenching, devastating, heartbreaking vulnerability blanketed the room. From the surgeon, laying bare his heart, this failure. From me, my child, my love, who mere days ago had been safe inside my womb.

Numbness claimed my heart. But from the tremendous courage and vulnerability the surgeon was not obligated to offer us, truth arose to meet Truth. With barely a conscious thought, I heard the Advocate quietly flow across my lips; "We do not need you to ask us for forgiveness. What happened will be revealed; but until then, we need you to forgive yourself. Other children need your skills and training. You cannot let this keep you from helping them. Remember this, learn from this, forgive yourself, so it won't happen again."

In the most vulnerable moment of my life, I didn't choose these words, but the Spirit of Truth within revealed my truest prayer. Eight years later, I am still in awe at the ways the Holy was present. I do not want to repeat that day. I do not wish this heartbreaking, heart-opening on anyone. And yet, on this side of some hard-fought healing, I can't help but long for more of God's holy clarity.

Is it possible to be open to God in the everyday? The times in traffic or when a friend comes for dinner to share in daily bread? Am I aware of the Spirit's presence enough to be vulnerable like Mary, daily offering my truest self? I pray for the courage to live this truth every day *and* the big moments.

Prayer: Gentle Spirit, you walk with us daily. In the pick-up line or the grocery store, attune our hearts to your tender word. May we become your Spirit of Truth. Amen.

—Rev. Robyn Bles

Unconditional Grace

While he was at Bethany in the house of Simon the leper, as he sat at the table, a woman came with an alabaster jar of very costly ointment of nard, and she broke open the jar and poured the ointment on his head. (Mark 14:3, NRSV)

It is a great injustice that we never learn the name of this woman in this gospel of Mark. There is no better example in scripture of what it means to be vulnerable and the unconditional grace that walks alongside vulnerability. She gets what it means to embrace the way of God as known through Jesus.

She sees the storm clouds gathering around Jesus. She senses that the Roman Empire would find some way to accost him. This is *the* time for a sacred moment of grace. She knows this is what is needed at this moment. She breaks open the expensive jar of nard. She knows that everyone will know what she did, even before she anoints Jesus, because nard is so pungent. Others would immediately notice and make their own judgment about what she was doing. She puts herself out there, and in her vulnerability, we experience the unconditional grace of God. She knows that grace is priceless. She knows what is truly sacred and recognizes there is always enough to go around. Through her actions, we are reminded of this truth.

Prayer: Gracious God, thank you for the witness of this unnamed woman. Help us to be vulnerable enough to recognize the moments when our faith calls us to be vulnerable enough to trust in you and your way, which is the way of grace. Amen.

—Rev. Daniel B. Gulden

Savoring Vulnerable Moments

A woman came to Jesus with an alabaster jar of very costly ointment, and she poured it on his head as he sat at the table. But when the disciples saw it, they were angry and said, "Why this waste?" But Jesus said to the disciples, "Why do you trouble the woman? What she has done will be told in remembrance of her." (Matthew 26:7, 8, 10, 13b, NRSV)

Jesus holds our gaze here—in this moment—to savor our foremother's generosity. And we remain transfixed even today by her display of tender vulnerability, and her challenge to the status quo of societal norms. For indeed, she is a woman who shocks the sensibilities of male disciples in Ancient Mesopotamia.

Jesus elevates her generosity as she anoints his head with oil through abundant praise—"What she has done will also be told in remembrance of her" (Matthew 26:13b). Her story—her actions—constitute a resonant legacy through the annals of Christian consciousness and, perhaps, invite our modern sensibilities to pause and reflect on lavish moments of vulnerability we might have otherwise overlooked.

What would our lives look like if we celebrated vulnerability in our everyday lives as sacred ... even holy? How might we live differently if we relished these vulnerable acts as if they were meant to honor our own journey and story?

Prayer: Jesus, who turns our eyes to the small intimate moments of vulnerability we might have otherwise overlooked, we give thanks for the examples of our beloved foremother and teacher in this passage. We give thanks for her challenge to the status quo, and we give thanks to her radical witness of vulnerable, abundant love. May we prepare our eyes and hearts to receive the blessings of vulnerability in our own journeys and extend them to others in return. Amen.

—Rev. Christian Watkins

Unashamed Love

... you anoint my head with oil; my cup overflows. (Psalm 23:5, NIV)

In my experience of oil, a little bit goes a long way. Whether used for cooking, revitalizing your hair, maintaining farm equipment, or preventing chapped lips, oil quickly spreads, covers, and protects.

Psalm 23 is all about trust, teaching how God uses oil abundantly in anointing each of us, abundantly covering us. And oh, how it takes vulnerability to trust in others, including God.

The gesture of anointing is typically saved for an honored guest or coronating a royal, not for normal people like you and me. And yet, God sees us for who we are, worthy, and does something about it—anointing us with the oil of abundance and unashamed love, daily seizing the opportunity to express love for us. Thus, reminding us that indeed we are worth such extravagance, such abundance. A faithful display of God's whole self being poured out for us. A revealing of God's vulnerability with us and for us. A reminder of how we are to live daily like God.

Prayer: May we freely pour ourselves out so completely in the giving of ourselves to God, that others might notice and do the same.

—Rev. Cassie Sexton

WEEK 4

Embrace

Spiritual Practice Invitation:

Practice a Loving-Kindness meditation (find a guide here: https://jackkornfield.com/meditation-lovingkindness).

At the beginning of each week, you will be invited to explore a spiritual practice in rhythm with the theme of the week. Consider adopting this practice for the week or the entire season.

Embracing Ourselves, Embracing One Another

Now that I, your Lord and Teacher, have washed your feet, you also should wash one another's feet. (John 13:14, NIV)

Leonardo da Vinci's *The Last Supper* is one of my favorite paintings, even if I don't think it's historically accurate. In my mind's eye, people of all backgrounds, ages, style, and gender were present, leaning in to hear Jesus, whose skin and hair are dark. More than the twelve, I imagine a room full of people eating food, sharing stories, and gossiping. What I love about da Vinci's painting is all of the leaning, the gesturing, the embracing, the whispering, and the wonder of this moment and shared meal.

During my congregation's own interpretation of the Last Supper during Maundy Thursday worship service, we ignored the trend to invite folks to wash the less intimate hands of one another, and invited them into the vulnerability of washing feet.

As I sang in the choir, I was moved to tears watching strangers and friends alike lean down, take off the shoes of the person in front of them, place that person's feet in the warmed water, and then embrace one another. One couple came forward, a woman taking the seat, a man leaning down to take off her sandals. After forty years of life together, they washed each other's feet for the first time as husband and wife, one having transitioned his gender during the previous year. At their embrace of one another and their complex, loving history, I wiped tears as I added their faces to *The Last Supper* of my imagination.

Prayer: God of love and tender touch, embrace us in our complexities and allow us to make room for each other as you make room for us. Amen.

—Rev. Lauren Bennett

Staying Present When Words Fail

So the sisters sent word to Jesus, "Lord, the one you love is sick ... Where have you laid him?" he asked. "Come and see, Lord," they replied. Jesus wept. Then the Jews said, "See how he loved him!" (John 11:3, 34–36, NIV)

When I worked as a hospital chaplain in the ICU, I learned how quickly I reach for stock phrases with grieving people. True or not, statements like, "God has a plan," "everything happens for a reason," or, worse still, "try to look on the bright side" usually land wrong. We know this somehow, but we still feel like we have to say something, don't we? That impulse to speak, while understandable, often stems from our own discomfort. If we aren't careful, we end up speaking out of a need to alleviate our own sense of anxiety in a way that imposes a cost on the person we're supposed to be attending.

Many words are injected in the surrounding passage, but at the precise moment Jesus steps into the room where Lazurus had died, the Lord was without speech: He simply wept. The reality is that words sometimes fail us: Some losses will never "make sense." In situations like these, our most faithful response is often a wordless presence that communicates everything it needs to. Embracing our own difficult emotions and staying close to hurting people, without projecting anxiety or judgment, this is faithful ministry that our world desperately needs.

Prayer: Precious Jesus, be close beside me in my own moments of pain. Teach me to embrace my own difficult emotions. Bring me a peace that passes understanding. Make me an instrument of your peace. Help me to stay present with those who are grieving, especially when words fail. Amen.

—Rev. Ross Allen

Staying in the Room

When Jesus saw her weeping, and the Jews who came with her also weeping, he was greatly disturbed in spirit and deeply moved. (John 11:33, NRSV)

I remember serving as a hospital chaplain and responding to a CPR code in the emergency room. The patient's husband was anxiously waiting in the family room when his husband died. I entered the room with the doctor when the news was given and was met with a horrifying scream that erupted from the husband's mouth.

The doctor immediately left the room, but I stayed and witnessed the erupting pain and grief that was flowing from his loss. I stayed with him for an hour, allowing him to express his grief, but I fully admit that my heart was broken, and I was so disturbed by the experience that I returned to my desk weeping.

A month later, the husband returned to the hospital unexpectedly, only to thank me for the care he had received that day. That experience reminds me of Jesus being greatly disturbed in spirit from the outpouring grief he witnessed from Mary and Martha, and how he cared for them despite allowing himself to be vulnerable from his compassion.

Prayer: Loving God, may our compassion lead us toward healing acts of comfort toward others who may be sitting in the ashes of grief, suffering, and despair. And may our vulnerability through compassion lead us toward connection with the broken-hearted. Amen.

—Rev. Kevin Toth

Trees

I see people. They look like trees, only they are walking around. (Mark 8:22–26, NIV)

Jesus meets a man who is blind. The pair walk to the outskirts of the city, where Jesus attempts to heal the man with a combination of dust from the earth and spit from his mouth. The salve, however, doesn't work to heal the man completely. He tells the miracle worker that he can see people, but they look like trees.

Imagine saying something so truthful to Jesus. If I were in his place, I would have said, "Yes, Lord! I see perfectly," so as not to have taken any more of the Lord's time. Not this man. This man dares to tell the truth of his incomplete healing. He doesn't try to avoid the truth of his discomfort to make another feel comfortable. He is not satisfied with his half-healed life because he knows those are people, not trees. He is honest enough to say what others might not. Being honest with oneself is an act of love. *So, Jesus, one more moment, please...*

Self-compassion can take many forms. In this story, it takes shape in the man's honesty about his vision. *I see, but I do not see perfectly.* I read this story and think of friends who've also dared to tell the truth about their lives. They've loved themselves enough to know they deserve more—a higher wage for their work, a therapist and medication, a church that affirms their humanity, a break, a sabbatical.

The man says to Jesus, "Here is my truth." And Jesus says. "Let's do it again."

Prayer: God of Truth, some truths need to be shared. Help us to tell the truth about our half-healed lives. You meet us there with your truth: You are my beloved. Amen.

—Rev. Nathan Kibler

Holding It Together

Jesus said to [Martha], "Did I not tell you that if you believed you would see the glory of God?" (John 11:40, NIV)

This is one of those stories where you know the ending before you know the details. Lazarus was raised from the dead. Though upon careful reading, I see this is not actually a story about Lazarus. This is a story about the faith of his sisters.

In their interactions with Jesus, both sisters say that if he had gotten there sooner, their brother would not have died. The sisters and Jesus know death didn't have to be the end of Lazarus's story. Martha tells Jesus she knows he is the Messiah. Jesus offers words of hope that Lazarus will be raised from the dead. Mary weeps and lets Jesus weep with her. They are in this together.

Faith is something we hold in community. We are part of churches and small groups and Sunday School classes because learning together deepens our understanding. We are better equipped for moments when faith doesn't come easily when we surround ourselves with a community who will do the heavy lifting when we can't do it ourselves. Mary and Martha held their faith together for Lazarus, and they all reaped the rewards of resurrection.

Prayer: Holy One, you have brought us together into communities so we may find joy and delight in companionship with one another and with you. Help us to be faithful in community so that we can care for each other well, holding the gift and challenge of faith together with gentleness. Amen.

—Rev. Kelsey Cobbs

Transforming Ourselves, Transfiguring Our World

The [reign] of God is among you. (Luke 17:21b, NRSV)

In this beloved scripture, Jesus reminds his followers that the reign of God is not some otherworldly place of eternal comfort, but a hoped-for reality in the here and now in which peace triumphs, justice for the marginalized prevails, and compassion permeates all life.

The traditional interpretation that the reign of God is "within us"—although a less accurate translation—is also true. Our Buddhist siblings remind us that if we are really going to transform the world, we must begin with ourselves. The kind of world about which Jesus spoke begins by caring for our own spirits. We cannot craft a peaceful world if we are not at peace with ourselves. We cannot create justice for others while bearing the weight of oppression. We cannot be compassionate toward others if we have not first been compassionate toward ourselves. Today, let's care for ourselves so that we can also transfigure this world that God loves.

Prayer: Source of Inner Light and Outer Radiance, may we tend to the growth of our spirits, so that we might cultivate a kinder, gentler world. May it be so. Amen.

—Rev. Caleb Lines

WEEK 5

Connect

Spiritual Practice Invitation:

Call someone you haven't spoken with in a while.
Ask them how you can be praying with them.
Pray with them.

At the beginning of each week, you will be invited to explore a spiritual practice in rhythm with the theme of the week. Consider adopting this practice for the week or the entire season.

Connect

Now as they went on their way, he entered a certain village, where a woman named Martha welcomed him into her home. (Luke 10:38, NRSV)

"A woman named Martha." You and I are introduced to Martha in this scripture passage, but Jesus has known her for years. They are family friends, with a history and a knowing. I imagine them playing in the dirt as children, making mischief together as teenagers, arms wrapped around each other's shoulders in moments of grief when a comforting presence is what is most needed. Jesus knows Martha well, along with her sister Mary and her brother Lazarus. He is part of their "village" of friends.

Luke introduces us to Martha for the first time here. Perhaps this is why when we read this scripture passage, we often give their relationships an introductory-level meaning. Martha is a resentful workaholic. Mary is oblivious to her sister's efforts of hospitality. Martha gets the work done (like so many church volunteers), while Mary listens to the prophet in their midst (we're doing that in church too, right?). They are action and stillness, hospitality and welcome. And ... Jesus knows they are so much more.

Can you recall a time when you felt truly known by another person? When you were seen in the fullness of your being—imperfections, distracted tendencies, bad habits and all—and *loved* so well that the good in you is what that person saw more than anything else? Maybe even loved so well that they could speak truth to you in a way that called you back to being your best self? How might you find, build, or seek relationships and communities of such depth and love?

Prayer: Beloved, search my heart and know me well. Laugh with me in my tendencies to distraction, my avoidance techniques. Then call me back to my most real and true self. Call me back to my love for you. Invite me to rest in your presence and be renewed for the work you call me to in the world.

—Rev. Melanie Harrell Delaney

House Calls

Now Simon's mother-in-law was in bed with a fever, and they told [Jesus] about her at once. He came and took her by the hand and lifted her up. (Mark 1:30–31, NRSV)

In Mark's gospel, Jesus' first healing is for Simon's (who is not yet Peter) mother-in-law. Jesus and the first disciples begin their ministry close to home in Capernaum, where Jesus preaches, exorcises an unclean spirit, and then go to Simon's home. There they find his mother-in-law in bed with a fever.

It has already been a full day. Nevertheless, Jesus takes her by the hand. He lifts her up. The fever is gone.

The cynic might see self-interest in this first healing: After all, Simon's mother-in-law rises and begins serving them. Perhaps all they really wanted was lunch.

That could be. But I also see an important beginning. Jesus will be the master physician, but at this moment, he's just making a house call. We all have to start somewhere, and Jesus chooses to begin his healing ministry close to home with a loved one of his new friend.

Perhaps it is still the case that the best place to begin our work is with our beloveds who are close by, that house calls are still where miracles happen, and that healing starts when we grab another by the hand.

Prayer: God of Here and There, keep my senses attuned to where I am and who I am with. Give me the courage to start right where I am, even as I participate in your coming family which has no limits. Amen.

—Rev. Colton Lott

You Are Seen

He was in the wilderness forty days, tested by Satan, and he was with the wild beasts, and the angels waited on him. (Mark 1:13 NRSVUE)

Since Ash Wednesday, we've been with Jesus in the wilderness where, as Mark succinctly describes, Jesus dwelt with dangerous and unpredictable animals and was tempted by Satan.

As Jesus faced these serious physical and spiritual menaces, angels waited on him.

We, too, are surrounded by angels. As we thump our way through the construction zone, the highway worker assures our safe passage. As we agonize through another major life transition, our parent reminds us who we always have been. A bank teller patiently resets our ATM password *again*. A nurse eases our worry. A friend watches from the car until we cross our threshold. An usher hands us a cough drop. Our weather forecaster, therapist, store clerk, favorite auntie ... all are angels among us.

From the time our waking feet search for their cozy slippers until the time we kick off the slippers to slide back under our blankets, a thousand things must go right. Much of what gets us through our day springs from positive actions of other humans.

Angels waited on Jesus. The word describing those angelic ministrations shares the same root as our English word, "deacon." As Jesus followers, we are called to serve others, but human connections flow many directions. We, too, are served. We, too, are cared for. We, too, are seen.

Prayer: Dear God, unstop my ears, open my eyes, and tune my heart to perceive the luminous array of angels surrounding me today. Amen.

—Rev. Amy Lignitz Harken

Too Much to Do!

But Martha was distracted by her many tasks ... (Luke 10:40 NRSV)

Martha and I have a lot in common. Whenever I am working on a project at the church, I spend the majority of my time formulating a list of tasks that must be accomplished so everything will run smoothly. One Sunday, I had baptized one of my church youth; after the baptism, he came up to me and asked me to join him and his family for lunch to continue celebrating his special day. However, I had a very long to-do list that needed to be completed, so I told him I was unable to join. I could see the look of disappointment on his face, and he wasn't the only one. In that moment, I remembered that my to-do list, while important, was distracting me from my calling as a minister: to build relationships and foster love and care with my youth.

Tasks are a natural part of life, and we will never be rid of them. Yet, Jesus reminds us through Martha that our relationships are essential to our lives and should not be taken away by our tasks. I appreciate this reminder as I work on not allowing the tasks and distractions to keep me from these blessed relationships of meaning and grace.

Prayer: Holy God, may the tasks in our lives not cause separation in our relationships, and may we create space to fully be present with one another with open hearts and minds. Amen.

—Rev. Kevin Toth

Martha's House

As they went on their way, he entered a certain village, where a woman named Martha welcomed him into her home. (Luke 10:38 NRSV)

"Martha welcomed him into her home." Ah, the gift of hospitality. A few verses earlier, Jesus said, "Foxes have holes, and birds of the air have nests, but the Son of Man has nowhere to lay his head" (Luke 9:48). But he knows he is welcome at Martha's house. There he can lay down his weary head.

Thanks be to God for Marthas, people whose homes and hearts are open to sojourners. Robert Frost once said, "Home is the place where when you have to go there, they have to take you in." Martha's house is the place where, when you have nowhere else to go, you know you will be welcomed.

Would that every church be Martha's House Christian Church: a welcoming sanctuary in a world predisposed to judgment, a house of refuge where runaways from hurtful circumstances are received with mercy and grace.

Prayer: Gracious God, make my church a Martha's house, a safe, welcoming place for everyone on the journey of faith and life.

—Rev. David Shirey

Las Atrevidas

When one of the Pharisees invited Jesus to have dinner with him, he went to the Pharisee's house and reclined at the table. A woman in that town who lived a sinful life learned that Jesus was eating at the Pharisee's house, so she came there with an alabaster jar of perfume. As she stood behind him at his feet weeping, she began to wet his feet with her tears. Then she wiped them with her hair, kissed them and poured perfume on them. (Luke 7:36–50 NIV)

In the earliest times in Colombian culture, a woman who dared to approach and speak directly to a man could be called *La atrevida* (the daring). Even more so in first-century culture in the village of Bethany—where Jesus had an encounter with Mary, who sat at his feet, and an unnamed woman who anointed Jesus' feet—the situation was somewhat similar. That is to say, in the village of Bethany, two different women were *Las atrevidas*.

Las atrevidas are those women who disrupt the masculine patriarchal spaces, fixed religious-cultural spaces, and rigid institutions. Both Mary and the unnamed woman *se atreven* (they dare). Sitting at Jesus' feet and anointing him is an effective subversion because they are quietly but visibly taking up space they are not "supposed" to occupy as women.

In this in-between space of the named woman and the unnamed woman, an ethic of disruption breaks the routine and calls any assumption into question by putting these two women at the center. Isn't that more important than Martha's worries, without undermining her hospitable spirit? After all, isn't that the gospel of God's kin-dom in the midst of the daily *luchas* (struggles) of women today?

Prayer: At your feet, oh God, we come to pray for those women who are *atrevidas*. Bless them with your perfume of love and kindness. Amen

—Rev. Néstor A. Gómez

Distracted

But the Lord answered her, "Martha, Martha, you are worried and distracted by many things..." (Luke 10:41, NRSV)

When reading scripture aloud, tone and pace makes such a difference in our understanding. For example, why does Jesus say Martha's name twice in this sentence? Depending on how it's read, it could radically change the meaning. Is he annoyed? Is he shaking his head, rolling his eyes, like, "Seriously, why don't you get this?"

I used to think so. Then I became a parent.

Now I realize that sometimes you need to repeat someone's name a couple of times to disconnect their attention from their preoccupation, and connect it to what you're saying to them. I think that's what Jesus is doing here.

Jesus knows how distracted Martha is with her own certainty about her "many tasks." In order to grasp her attention and turn her toward presence, toward relationship, he needs to repeat her name until he has her focus.

I could be wrong, but I also get where Martha is here. It's hard for me to be thoughtfully present when I've got a to-do list piling up in my head. I worry about forgetting something important, so I want to start knocking those tasks out. Then I can then relax and get on with my day. But Jesus is seeing Martha and me more like we're the kids in class with our hands in the air, offended by how long it's taking the teacher to call on us, annoyed that we have to wait for inferior thoughts to be shared. *Put your hand down, Martha (Mark). Just listen for a minute.*

We may need to be called by name—a couple of times—to disconnect us from our preoccupation, our ego, and to connect our attention to what's in front of us, to call us toward the better part.

Prayer: Holy One, you know our tendency toward overconfidence in our own certainty. Thank you for your patience with us, and for calling us, continually, to connect us. Amen.

—Rev. Mark Winters

WEEK 6

Awaken

Spiritual Practice Invitation:

Take a walk or look out a window.

Pay attention to what you notice.

Can you find anything you haven't seen before?

At the beginning of each week, you will be invited to explore a spiritual practice in rhythm with the theme of the week. Consider adopting this practice for the week or the entire season.

Awaken

They went and found a colt outside [Bethany] in the street, tied at a doorway. As they untied it, some people standing there asked, "What are you doing, untying that colt?" They answered as Jesus had told them to, and the people let them go. When they brought the colt to Jesus and threw their cloaks over it, he sat on it. Many people spread their cloaks on the road, while others spread branches they had cut in the fields. Those who went ahead and those who followed shouted, "Hosanna!" "Blessed is he who comes in the name of the Lord!" "Blessed is the coming kingdom of our father David!" "Hosanna in the highest heaven!" (Mark 11:4–10, NRSV)

This scripture has often given me great joy, just envisioning Jesus riding into his life's purpose on a colt. This was an act of humility and strength. Knowing the same crowd now shouting hosanna would soon change their shouts to crucify him, Jesus entered focused and unbothered.

A colt is known to be steadfast, stubborn, and laser focused (almost to a fault). I've wondered why Jesus requested a colt? They are not the most physically appealing animals. Yet, they can withstand what it means to travel on "tough and uncomfortable" long journeys.

On this Palm Sunday, where is your colt? Do you have something that holds you strong and faithful? We need that special something that will give us the ability to be awakened from darkness and defeat. Where is your donkey? What will push you beyond the struggle to experience the hope and joy of Jesus?

Prayer: Lord, where is my donkey? Let my eyes see, may my heart feel and my feet move. May I be awakened to power and purpose. Amen.

—Rev. Dr. Darren Phelps

New Vision

And many spread their clothes on the road, and others cut down leafy branches from the trees and spread them on the road. (Mark 11:8, KJV)

There are times we only see things for what they are or the way we know them to be of use. As I consider this, there are numerous scriptures that come to mind: when Moses' staff was used to divide the sea, when the oil was used to pay off debts.

In this text we see how palm branches and cloaks were used to create a red carpet of sorts, as Jesus made his way into Jerusalem. The people were so excited about his arrival and were willing to use the very clothes off their backs to ensure Jesus received a proper welcome. They came together and used what they had.

We don't always think we have enough, if anything at all, to show people kindness. As a result, we shy away from opportunities. However, most times, we have more than we think.

A week ago, a young lady reached out to me about housing. The places I would have recommended to her, she'd already contacted, to no avail. I got a divine nudge to post the request on Facebook. I was hesitant but did it anyway.

Some time passed and I hadn't received any notifications for the post. If I'm honest, I felt a bit discouraged. More time passed and I received an inbox with a recommendation that led to the young lady receiving housing and funds to help her get through the week. Social media became a resource for more than just pictures and posts about life. It was a resource to help someone in need.

Prayer: Lord, give us a new vision to see the ways we can use what we have to show your love to others. Amen.

—Rev. Rae Karim

Awe

Many people spread their cloaks on the road, and others spread leafy branches that they had cut in the fields. (Mark 11:8, NRSV)

Last spring, our associate minister came back from a Bethany Fellows retreat and couldn't stop talking about "awe." Dacher Keltner defined it as, "the feeling of being in the presence of something vast that transcends your current understanding of the world."[3]

Awe can be found in the small things, like a beautiful sunny day. But it can also be found in something larger than ourselves, like the birth of a child or the remembrance of a life well lived.

When I read Mark's version of the Palm Sunday story, I can't help but wonder what it would have been like to witness Jesus' entry into Jerusalem. A man on a donkey—not a big parade, but a humble arrival—who inspired the people to lay down their cloaks like a red carpet. It was an experience that transcended their understanding of the world.

Have you been in awe lately?

Prayer: Holy One, as we journey through this Lenten season, let us not forget to ponder the world around us. Encourage us to stop, look and listen. We stand in awe of you. Amen.

—Rev. Kyle McDougall

[3] Dacher Keltner, *Awe* (New York: Penguin Press, 2023), 7.

Hard Sleeper

But [Jesus] was asleep in the stern, asleep on the cushion; and they woke him up... (Mark 4:35–41, NRSV)

When I was a child, I learned to wake my dad up from a nap by tapping on his calves. He spooks easily and generally rolls over with his arms flailing when he is woken up. It is best to keep distance from his upper body windmill.

When the storm was raging, I wonder how the disciples physically woke Jesus. Were they hollering? Was the wood beneath their feet clattering? Did they tap Jesus on the calf?

Jesus apparently woke up on the wrong side of the cushion. He chewed out the wind and the sea, and they got quiet pretty quickly. He then turned to the disciples, asking, "Why are you afraid? Have you still no faith?"

As we journey through this Holy Week, we will inevitably be asked if *we* are awake. We so easily assume that we must be the ones asleep while Jesus is always wide awake. But it is not always so; once the familiar script was flipped.

Good news: We can wake Jesus up. But beware. He might be grumpy and come out swinging. He might just ask why we were afraid in the first place, why we still have no faith.

Prayer: God of work and rest, help us to do our part of faith so that storms are stilled and our trust in you is unable to be washed away. Amen.

—Rev. Colton Lott

Jumping Off

This is because the foolishness of God is wiser than human wisdom, and the weakness of God is stronger than human strength. (1 Corinthians 1:25, NRSV)

"I pity the fool." The famous words of Mr. T. ring true these decades on. We look at foolish people with (at best) pity. Usually, it comes closer to derision. We see people of weak stature as "less than." Whether we admit it or not, everyone wants a person or someone we can look down upon. No one wants to be on the lowest rung of the societal ladder.

We're always trying to climb to the top of some type of ladder: the corporate ladder, the good-parent ladder, the appropriately concerned ladder, the health ladder, the prayer ladder. Desperately climbing hand over fist, we cling to the hope that all our work, struggle, and striving will pay off when we reach the top. But even if we make it to some self-made pedestal, we find there's always higher to climb. The ladder ends up being more like a hamster wheel.

What would happen if you were to jump off? Forsake the rat race? Give up? You would probably be called a fool. You might be thought of as weak. But that's okay, because you'll awaken to find those same attributes make you just God's cup of tea.

Prayer: Gracious God, awaken us once again to the truth that your ways are not our ways, and that is a good thing. Amen.

—Rev. Will Ryan

What It Takes to Open Up

Open to me the gates of righteousness, that I may enter through them and give thanks to the Lord. (Psalm 118:19, NRSV)

My family used to drive up to Maine each spring to open our summer cottage. When we'd arrive, the uninsulated cabin in the woods would be covered in pine needles left from the fall and winter months. My dad would stand on the low roof, sweeping these needles away. It was hard work to open up the cottage, a chore my parents probably didn't look forward to. There were mice and cobwebs, but we knew we had to prepare the space for all the adventures that would await us in the summer.

I think about how difficult it is for us to open up, to share the deepest parts of ourselves, to be vulnerable, to trust. The tulip bulbs that waited all winter which now poke their heads through the dirt make it look so easy. But it was hard work for them, too. Whether it's sweeping away injustice or opening up to deeper understanding, we too are waking up and shedding what no longer serves us in this season.

Prayer: God whose love endures forever, even in these days we pray that you would help us oil the hinges of the gates of our hearts. Help us sweep away the cobwebs of all that holds us back from being who you call us to be. Amen.

—Rev. Emelia Attridge

Be Kind, Rewind

And you shall know that I am the Lord, when I open your graves, O my people. I will put my spirit within you, and you shall live ... (Ezekiel 37:13–14a, NRSV)

It's no secret that I have a love of words. But it's not just the creation of prose I love—it's editing. It's the process of ripping apart the old and ushering in the new. Rearranging, reworking, changing, and transforming what we already have to bring a newer, clearer, beautiful life to it.

My favorite part of ministry is holding hope and energy for future possibilities. I often hear the refrain from Ezekiel 37:11b, "Our bones are dried up and our hope is gone; we are cut off." The pain of editing and awakening new possibilities is recognizing the current reality.

It's getting comfortable with the uncomfortable.

It's fostering constructive struggle.

And then it's a slow sewing together of sinew and flesh, of healing from the damages now recognized. Allowing ourselves to awake is a raw experience of the holy. It's a reworking of what's been created in sacredness.

Prayer: Editing God, show us all the beauty surrounding us, give us new eyes to see, and awaken us to a new dawn. Amen.

—Rev. Aerii Smith

Assured

The women hurried away from the tomb, afraid yet filled with joy, and ran to tell his disciples. Suddenly Jesus met them. "Greetings," he said. They came to him, clasped his feet and worshiped him. (Matthew 28:8–9, NRSV)

Often on Easter Sunday, the walking iris at the bottom of the stairs at the main entrance of the church is in bloom. Each bloom opens for one day before closing in on itself and soon falling into the soil. On that day, the weight of the flower draws the stem to the ground, each bloom drawing it nearer and nearer to the dirt, where eventually the plant is able to root and propagate.

I wonder if the iris has any fear as it chooses its day to bloom. Does it choose to weigh down the stem knowing it will be seen by passersby wanting to stop and snap a photo or bend to smell its sweet fragrance? Do other blooms wait for a day the church is likely to be unoccupied, enjoying the quiet solitude, to bend toward the soil? Do the blooms even have a choice at all, or are they just surprised with life?

The women who tell the story of life, *afraid yet filled with joy*, don't seem to have much choice. They witness an unbelievable thing, meet with the most ordinary of greetings, and do the most extraordinary act: They believe their experience and run to tell the others. They draw near to the miracle and invite the community to participate. They are assured of the wonder of life generating life; they bloom into action assured of their place in the greater family of things.

What is blooming in your life? What fragrances are drawing you near? What is your part in the family of things?

Prayer: Living God, open us to new possibilities. Assure us we can bloom. Guide us to the fragrance of other blooms. Bend our wills toward the soil. Amen.

—Rev. Lauren Bennett

Resilient

When he had led them out to the vicinity of Bethany, he lifted up his hands and blessed them. While he was blessing them, he left them and was taken up into heaven. Then they worshiped him and returned to Jerusalem with great joy. And they stayed continually at the temple, praising God. (Luke 24:50–53 NIV)

As we celebrate the resurrection of Jesus, we are invited to pause and ponder, to focus on the strength and ability to withstand trials. Through the life of Christ, we now have joy unspeakable. The Monday after is when we proclaim that the holy doors of the living sanctuary will remain open to all! It symbolizes that heaven has been opened as Christ has returned.

What happened on Easter Monday? There is no specific record of events taking place on Easter Monday, but it does begin Jesus' forty days on earth before the Lord ascended to heaven. During this time, Jesus appeared to believers, healed the sick, and shared the living word of God.

As Luke 24:50–53 joyfully reminds us, the Monday after we are called to a place of groundedness, faith, and courage. It is here that we hold fast the prayers of Jesus and the promise of "goodness" to follow us through our journey—that the joy of the Lord will fulfill our desire to honor God with our lives.

From our rest, we have learned to listen; to lean in to vulnerability and embrace the full range our being; to connect more deeply with God, ourselves, and others; to see the stories of our lives and the resources around us with new eyes; and to be inspired and called to partner with God in active, world-changing ways. Thanks be to God for the way of Jesus Christ—from rest to resilience!

Prayer: Lord, on this Monday after, may we forever celebrate your life! May we hold close the meaning and power of the resurrection. Let our faith in you create in us an unwavering resilience!

—Rev. Dr. Darren Phelps

Contributors

Rev. Ross M. Allen is the minister of South Acton Congregational Church in Acton, Massachusetts.

Rev. Emelia Attridge is settled minister of First Congregational Church of Reading, United Church of Christ, in Reading, Massachusetts.

Rev. Lauren Bennett is pastor at Metropolitan Community Church of Greater St. Louis.

Rev. Robyn M. Bles is the senior minister of Wakonda Christian Church in Des Moines, Iowa.

Rev. Kelsey Cobbs is the minister of Federated Church of Weatherford in Western Oklahoma, affiliated with the Disciples of Christ, Presbyterian Church (USA), and United Church of Christ.

Rev. Tiffany Curtis is founding pastor of The Open Circle in Santa Fe, New Mexico.

Rev. Melanie Harrell Delaney is co-director/pastor of Bethany Fellows.

Rev. Dr. Néstor Gómez is lead pastor of First Congregational Church in Stamford, Connecticut, and a Bethany Fellows mentor/leader.

Rev. Danny Gulden is lead minister at Geist Christian Church in Fishers, Indiana.

Rev. Dr. Amy Lignitz Harken is an interim minister in Maine.

Rev. Courtney Hickman is associate minister at First Christian Church in Wilmington, North Carolina.

Rev. Rae Karim is the founder of Good Grief Now!™, a grief support organization.

Rev. Nathan Kibler is senior minister at Central Christian Church in Lebanon, Indiana.

Rev. Sarah Kingsbery is a hospital chaplain and a congregational consultant on stewardship.

Rev. Jack Knox is senior minister of First Christian Church of Lufkin, Texas.

Rev. Cheryl Russell Kunkel is associate regional minister in the Christian Church (Disciples of Christ) in Indiana.

Rev. Caleb J. Lines is senior minister of University Christian Church in San Diego, California.

Rev Colton D. Lott is the pastor of First Christian Church in El Reno, Oklahoma.

Rev. Dr. Sarah Lund is senior pastor of First Congregational United Church of Christ in Indianapolis, Indiana.

Rev. Steve Mason is the pastor of First Christian Church in Canton, Illinois.

Rev. Kyle McDougall is associate minister at First Christian Church in Bowling Green, Kentucky.

Rev. Larry J. Morris, III, is the executive director/lead pastor of the Inclusive Collective in Chicago.

Rev. Sara Wilcox Patty is an alumna of the Bethany Disciple Fellows.

Rev. Dr. Darren Phelps is community regional minister of the Christian Church (Disciples of Christ) Southwest Region, and a Bethany Fellows mentor/leader.

Rev. Seth Rash is the associate minister of youth and family at First Christian Church in Troy, Missouri.

Rev. Will Ryan is senior minister at First Christian Church in Fulton, Missouri.

Rev. Cassie Sexton-Riggs is senior pastor at Union Avenue Christian Church in Litchfield, Illinois.

Rev. David Shirey is a retired pastor in the Christian Church (Disciples of Christ) and a longtime Bethany Fellows mentor/leader.

Rev. Aerii Smith is senior pastor at First Christian Church in Cheyenne, Wyoming.

Rev. Casey Tanguay is the pastor of WestWind Church (Disciples of Christ) in Keller, Texas.

Rev. Kevin Toth is associate minister at First Christian Church in Crawfordsville, Indiana.

Rev. Isaac Varner, minister at Independence Christian Church in Ashland, Virginia.

Rev. Christian Watkins is executive director and campus minister at Ecumenical Campus Ministries at Kansas State University.

Rev. Tiff Williams is the senior pastor of Rush Creek Christian Church in Arlington, Texas.

Rev. Mark Winters is pastor of Federated Church of Martha's Vineyard in Edgartown, Massachusetts.

About Bethany Fellows

Bethany Fellows supports congregations and communities by inspiring and sustaining pastors in their earliest years of ministry. Bethany Fellows helps newly ordained, young pastors transition from seminary to sustained ministry with well-being and strength of spirit. In 1999, when Bethany Fellows began, almost 40% of young clergy left ministry due to burn-out, loneliness, or financial strain. For 25 years and with over 200 alumni, we celebrate that 90% of Bethany Fellows pastors and alumni are still in ministry, with 70% serving congregations. Bethany Alumni and congregations credit "The Bethany Way" of prayer, vulnerability, and connection for their thriving.

The Bethany Disciple Fellows and Bethany Ecumenical Fellows groups serve up to 70 young pastors each year in a four-year rhythm of retreats, mentors, and spiritual practices. While on retreat, Fellows receive the prayerful support of experienced pastors/mentors, encouragement of significant collegial relationships, and visits with dynamic congregations and faith leaders, fueling creativity and inspiration to share with the Fellows' own congregations. Through Bethany Fellowships, young ministers are better able to navigate the beginnings of a pastoral vocation, as well as crucial young adult life transitions, building confidence and strengthening leadership. In 2021, Bethany Fellows launched Bethany Congregations, bringing congregational leaders and their pastor(s) into a Bethany experience of retreats, small groups, contemplative prayer, and wise practice conversations. Bethany Congregations nurtures resilience in discernment and action among congregational leadership teams and their wider communities.

Bethany Fellows is proudly rooted in the Christian Church (Disciples of Christ) and partners with Pension Fund of the Christian Church, facilitating the peer group component of Pension Fund's previous Excellence in Ministry and upcoming Cornerstones programs.

More information can be found at www.bethanyfellows.org or by contacting Rev. Melanie Harrell Delaney (Bethany Fellows Co-Director) at melanie@bethanyfellows.org, Rev. Kim Gage Ryan (Bethany Fellows Co-Director) at kim@bethanyfellows.org, or Bethany Congregations director Rev. Scott Hardin-Nieri at scott@bethanyfellows.org.

refusing today to join the huffing pack
chasing down the POET'S death
with their writing tools,
i've taken this crazy detour,
will not even write his name
        in defiance
        in deference

i bump into the POET
seated in a crummy luncheonette
in my poem, coffee & a bagel
with a smear of cream cheese
out of his Bronx boyhood,
that old floppy hat he wore in
San Francisco, day i met him
and we spent together;

bumming a cigarette, he winks at me
smiling flowers & children
all over my poem
wherever he sees gray,
making a toast:
    to life
    to life

LOOSELY ALONG ZEN LINES IT
IS

...everybody knows it's not
the tune that counts but IT...
Jack Kerouac (On The Road)

when someone in dirty clothes   torn shoes
stands on a street corner   in a crowded train
lifts his horn and blows
everyone to pieces

is

when a person i barely know
looks at me   nods at
what or who   our complicit yes / no

is

when this "pissed off East Village lady"
(as he called me)
angry at a guy i never met
who stood me up
flew out of the restaurant
and a man with a
gray pony tail   silver feather earring
leaning against a pole reading
looked up

is

when we met: on the inside/
only place we could survive

is

when my lover added
his body to mine
on someone's scratchy rug
one long New Jersey morning ago
one body   i saw only one

is

unconditional...like breathing
and knowing it   every breath

is

my mind stretched out in my body
down to the toes
taking in the sun one afternoon

is

IT

YES   absolutely

WHAT IT COMES DOWN TO

is breathing: a poem
every week   one body
strumming another on-
to the guitar   page...
to keep breathing
kept my ballet feet
outwitting pain longer than
they did   flying
off the ground   the word
to each other
what it all comes down to
everything came down too...
knew when I had it / absolutely
and when it broke
snapped like a band in my face
and flying off the page
was flying into a void
I knew   at any cost
getting back my breath
while still breathing,
what it now comes down to